WEST SUSSEX LIBRARY SERVICE	
201007649	
S820 HAN	WSL 7/15

Strawberries

Poems and short stories by Caroline Hansen

For Derek
with love and thanks

Acknowledgements

Thanks again to Sarah Higbee and the
Creative Writing Class at Northbrook College,
Morag Charlwood and the Portslade Writing Group,
and the Hurtspierpoint Association of Christian
Writers for their support, encouragement and
feedback.
Also to family, friends, and members of the Church
of the Good Shepherd, Shoreham Beach.

Index

A Matter of Taste

Beach Clean

Everyman

Fit for Purpose

Identity

Medina Maid

No Wheelchairs in Heaven

Requiem

Resolutions

Strawberries

The Devil You Know

The Quiet Road

A Matter of Taste

When they went to France he looked at the Carte.
"Steak tartare" he ordered "with frites."
"That will be fine, with a glass of red wine,
a rare and unusual treat."

She tried to warn him but it was too late.
When he looked at his plate of raw meat,
swallowing hard he knocked back his wine,
and decided to stick to the frites.

When they went to Spain she decided to ask
for the day's speciality dish.
The waiter declared, "Senora we have
the freshest of local caught fish."

With a flourish he left on their table a tray
of prawns, crab, mullet and bream.
As a lobster got up and started to walk,
she let out a terrified scream.

When they returned home they went out to eat
and both heaved a sigh of relief.
For there on the menu was sausage and mash,
fish and chips, and English roast beef.

Beach Clean

Alice was doing her morning beach clean. It was at first light before Shoreham Beach was awake and soon she would see the winter sunrise over the harbour. She loved this time of day. Apart from a few solitary dog walkers she was alone, with no interruption to her thoughts apart from the sound of the sea and the cries of the gulls.

As usual she scanned the beach for litter. Not so bad at this time of year, but the amount of debris that people just threw down never ceased to annoy her.

Every morning she would take her sack and fill it with bottles, cans, crisp packets and plastic bags. Saturday and Sunday mornings were the worst, especially in the summer, and she became really angry at the way picnickers would leave the remains of barbeques wherever they happened to be, even close to the various litter and recycling bins. She had collected odd shoes, swimsuits, and underwear as well as tennis balls, dog balls and footballs.

Broken bottles and other hazards were left heedlessly for small children to trip over, and she had seen car drivers in the summer let their dogs out to do their business, and then drive off without stepping out of their cars.

'*Bring back the wombles.*' She stopped to empty out the remainder of six cans of 'Special Brew', spilling some on her gloves as she stowed them in her plastic sack.

'*Now I shall smell like a brewery.*' Looking up she saw the sunrise, now a brilliant mixture of red and gold. A fishing boat was chugging along close to the shore and the skipper raised his hand in greeting as he passed her.

'*This is all so beautiful. Why do people have to spoil it?*' she asked herself for the thousandth time.

An all-year-round swimmer stopped to give her a cheery good morning as he wheeled his bike down to the rocks before plunging in for his early morning dip.

An unfamiliar figure was coming towards her. A young man with a red beanie hat, clutching a take-away coffee in one hand and what looked like a bacon sandwich in the other.

He had a large black dog trotting by his side who stopped to defecate. At that moment the wind caught the red hat blowing it towards the sea. Clasping his cup and sandwich he ran past, chasing the hat, cursing the wind and shouting at his dog to get out of the way as he ran round his master in excited circles.

He retrieved his beanie which had come to rest against a breakwater and made his way back up the beach. Alice's surprise must have showed clearly in her face as he retraced his steps, located his dog's mess, fished a plastic bag out of his pocket and bent down to clear it up.

He looked up at her. "You didn't expect me to do that did you?" The man smiled as he walked away.

Everyman

He'd tried hard to shape up since he was a boy
but somehow it kept going wrong.
"There's room for improvement," his father proclaimed.
"Try harder, don't leave it too long."

At school he was not at the bottom,
but neither was he near the top.
"There's room for improvement" his teachers all wrote.
"It's important standards don't drop."

When later he tried to start dating,
the girls wouldn't give him a chance.
"There's room for improvement," they giggled at him
whenever he asked them to dance.

At work he tried hard for promotion,
but somehow was always passed by.
"There's room for improvement" his bosses would say.
"Next year you can always retry"

Retiring he took up some hobbies,
joined classes and then a bowls club.
 "There's room for improvement" his friends all agreed
when they met afterwards in the pub

When old he became really poorly.
He lost all his get up and go.
 "There's room for improvement", the nurse said to him
as she helped him to walk to and fro.

When finally meeting St. Peter,
he didn't think he had a hope.
"There's room for improvement, I know it's the case,
I've never been able to cope."

Pearly gates opened wide as he entered,
Peter hugged him and said with a grin,
"You did all you could, to others been good.
You're a star. Take a harp and come in."

Fit for Purpose

I once knew a fat man, outside
a thin man who cried to get out.
He became very stressed,
and deeply depressed
because he'd become really stout.

He gave up puddings and pastries.
He gave up chocolates and wine.
He watched what he ate,
and tried to lose weight
to gain a sleek, sexy outline.

He took up running and swimming
and went every day to the gym.
He hoped to get lean
on the rowing machine,
determined he would be slim.

Changing from bread to Ryvita
he steered clear of biscuits and beer,
when hunger attacked
instead of a snack
he'd jog up and down Worthing pier.

One day he encountered his true love
and all augured well, until when
she said "I love you
but if I'm to be true,
I must tell you I hate skinny men."

He gave up running and swimming,
took his love wining, dining instead.
No longer depressed
he's not at all stressed,
and does his gymnastics in bed.

First published in The Shoreham and Worthing Herald, January 2014

Identity

Once I had
a name, address, and phone number,
driving licence, passport,
library ticket
and a cheque book.

In addition, I now have
 a credit card, debit card,
loyalty cards, bus pass,
European health insurance,
and a National Trust card.

Some time ago
the local branch of our bank
knew their customers by name.
Now a cash machine asks
me for my PIN number
from a hole in the wall.

I now have a mobile phone
with an impossibly long number,
and can text friends and family
so we don't need to talk.

I no longer have one name,
but several different 'user names'
and passwords, which
together with my PIN number
are all top secret,

I have an e-mail address
and answer security questions.
My favourite flowers,
my mother's maiden name,
my eldest child's second name,
the name of my first school,
so it can be checked
I am who I say I am.

If I forget who I am
I can go to Facebook,
to contact friends
who say they know me.

But I know who I am.
The same person who had
a name, address, and phone number,
driving licence, passport,
library ticket,
and a cheque book

Medina Maid

Getting the tide right was crucial so we set off at 2.30 a.m. from Poole Marina, both children still fast asleep in the forward cabin.

It was August 1981. This was our third year in our 27' yacht 'Medina Maid', and after some sailing holidays round the Solent and Poole Harbour, we needed a new engine. Now fitted with a new BMW diesel we prepared for the big adventure – from Portsmouth down to Dartmouth and Salcombe.

This was a challenge as the Portland Race, the waters off Portland Bill, can be treacherous and should be avoided particularly during spring tides.

On the morning the conditions were ideal, so we set off under motor close to the Old Harry Rocks, sheltered from the force 3-4 northerly wind for a calm passage to Portland Bill. At around 3.30 a.m. the engine spluttered and died.

Derek was the only experienced sailor on board. The children were still quite young, and I was a country girl at heart, and had never been sailing until I met Derek.

For six hours we tried to catch every puff of wind in the flapping sails to get out from the shelter of the cliffs, with intermittent efforts to restart the engine. The children now awake willingly set to, and we sang to keep our spirits up including several renditions of, 'For those in Peril on the Sea'. We had a ship's radio on board so why we didn't radio for help I cannot think, perhaps we were just too busy keeping clear of the rocks.

At last the sails filled and we were making headway. Unfortunately the tide had now turned against us which slowed us down, so it was around 2.30 p.m. (twelve hours since we had left Poole) before we reached the entrance to Weymouth Harbour.   We tacked into the harbour against the failing wind and the tide.

Another hour passed before we came up to the visitors moorings having struggled to get out of the way of the huge cross-channel ferry.

There was a lunch party on a large French yacht and we shouted for help to moor up. They put down their wine glasses and leapt enthusiastically into action.

At last we were safe.

James and Joanna, aged 13 and 11 had behaved brilliantly, no doubt realising that this was a genuinely perilous situation, but were less amenable when it came to the next four days stuck in one place while we waited for the engine to be repaired.

As it was the Friday before the Bank Holiday, it was Tuesday before an engineer appeared and fixed the engine so we could make our way onward to Dartmouth and Salcombe.

At Dartmouth, we celebrated our arrival by dining at Mr. Filthy McNasty's, an ideal location for the children, and I bought a weather forecast sweatshirt which I still have to this day.

No Wheelchairs in Heaven

There'll be no wheelchairs in heaven,
no specs, hearing aids, zimmer frames,
for we have been told new bodies await
the deaf, the blind and the lame.

There'll be no arthritis in heaven,
our muscles and joints will be free
of the aches and the pains, that inhibit us so
in hip, neck, shoulder or knee.

There'll be no diseases in heaven
of eye or body or brain,
and we all will be totally free
to live in a world without pain.

There'll be no medication in heaven
for those who are mentally ill,
just peace beyond understanding,
no need for injection or pill.

There'll be no competition in heaven
between women or men, young or old,
we'll all have such fun, together as one
as the joys that await us unfold.

There'll be no racial tension in heaven,
because there is simply no need.
Love will abound, enough to go round
regardless of colour or creed.

First published in Sea Breezes magazine Autumn 2013

Requiem

When you were young and I came down each morning
I'd say "Good Morning Lucy." You'd jump up
ready and eager to go out, to explore the day,
and find out all it held in store for us.

When you were old and sleepy I tickled you awake.
I lifted the flap of your ear and whispered,
"Who is the best dog in the world?"
You would rise and stretch and wag your tail.

Every evening you flirted with Derek,
dancing and twirling round on your bottom,
looking up with soulful brown eyes,
as he counted out and fed you treats.

You were so good, gentle and friendly to all,
but very greedy as spaniels often are.
I said "When you go off your food,
I'll know you're really ill, and start to worry."

Then you were sick and I took you to the Vet.
He tried antibiotics but you kept coughing.
You were in pain, your breathing laboured.
and no longer hungry, even for treats.

The last day I tickled you awake and whispered in your floppy ear, "Who's the best dog in the world?"

We stopped on the way to let you out of the car, to visit your favourite place at Sleepy Hollow. So you could go to sleep, still with the sights and smells fresh in your mind. The nearest thing to Doggy Heaven

We cried like babies when we said goodbye to Lucy,
Simply the "Best dog in the world"

Resolutions

It was New Year's Eve and the old year had ended with the same eight people seated round the dining table. They had just toasted the New Year in together as they had done for the last ten years.

As usual the conversation came round to resolutions. Jack their host started the ball rolling with "I'm not making any resolutions I can't keep, so I'm not making any." As always he laughed loudly at his own wit.

This was expected as he said the same thing every year. The others laughed dutifully, helped by a good meal, washed down with a plentiful supply of wine.

"How about you Helen?" Attention turned to Jack's long-suffering wife who not only heard the joke at the start of each year but on many other occasions in between.

"Oh you know, the usual things, take more exercise, lose weight, cut down on alcohol and fattening foods."

This brought sympathetic nods all round.

Mark said this was the year he was definitely going to give up smoking. He'd managed it once for six whole months only slipping back after a crisis at work.

Freddie, his partner, who didn't smoke, raised his eyebrows to heaven, and said if Mark didn't give up he had resolved to get out more, which brought a laugh from the others.

Sandy, voluble as ever, gave chapter and verse of all the ways she was going to be a better wife and mother. 'Never shout at the children. Get them away from television and computer games and make sure they spent time on outdoor pursuits. Spend quality time as a family. Bake more cakes for the school fete. Dispense with junk food and cook perfectly balanced meals. Smarten up her appearance. Make time to enquire about Tom's day when he came back from work,' . . . and would have continued but having caught sight of the others glazing over decided to finish there.

Tom's turn was next saying with a grin that in order to keep up with his 'about to be perfect wife' he thought he should join a gym, and go to evening classes to enable him to help the children with their homework which was rapidly becoming beyond his scope.

Attention turned to Ian and Jane, who looked at each other, neither wanting to speak first. Ian took a deep breath and said: "Jane and I have decided to go to America and join the Mennonites, so I'm sorry but this will be the last time we will be seeing in the New Year with you, our friends."

There was a stunned silence. Jack reached for the decanter of port. Mark delved in his pocket for his packet of cigarettes dodging Freddie who reached out to stop him. Helen grabbed at the dish of chocolates in the middle of the table, and Sandy and Tom suddenly realised that their baby-sitter had said she didn't want to be too late.

And the New Year had only just begun.

Retail Therapy

"Is it your turn or mine to take Rosie shopping?" I asked, deliberately vague.

"Definitely yours." Sally said in a tone that brooked no nonsense.

"I thought it might be," I knew she was right.

My sister and I took it in turns to take our mother shopping in the spring and autumn to buy her new clothes for the coming season. These were special outings, more challenging than the frequent trips to the local shops, or taking her to our own homes or out for coffee or lunch.

"I wondered if it might be better if we both went this time," I queried hopefully, "One to help select and try the dresses on, and the other to placate any shop assistants."

"Maybe you're right," she conceded, and I gave a sigh of relief.

Our mother, who we called by her Christian name, as we thought of her more as a child than a mother, had always been 'difficult,' and had become more so since our father died. We had always been told that she suffered with her nerves and we must make allowances. My friend Lizzie said that when people became older they reverted to childhood and asked if she had been spoiled or rebellious as a girl, which made me think back to stories Rosie had recounted with glee of how she put holly on her teacher's chair at school, and sneaked out to the cinema when she was supposed to be in bed, wearing a woolly hat as a disguise.

Sally and I set out on a Tuesday morning, not too early to give Rosie time to have her breakfast in bed and at least three cigarettes which she smoked hanging out of the window of her Care Home. She had been expelled from her last three Homes for disruptive behavior, but seemed to be settling in this one thanks to some extremely caring and understanding members of staff. I recalled with a sinking feeling the time when I picked up the phone from the last Care Home manager who said explosively, "I want your mother out of here as soon as you can find alternative accommodation." I asked him what had happened he just told me she was "impossible."

When I questioned Rosie, she was full of righteous indignation, and explained that all she had done was call out in the Dining Room a few times, "There goes the Tart," as one of the Care

Assistants went by, convinced she was having an affair with the manager, who was a married man.

It was a bright sunny morning and Sally drove. Rosie waved her stick about in the front pointing at other cars. "Did you see that driver cut in? That's my daughter's right of way. Road Hog."

She had never taken, let alone passed a driving test, and in the end I called out from the safety of the back seat. "You'll put Sally off her driving if you're not quiet," at which she reluctantly subsided. Sally dropped us off at the dress shop, carefully chosen over the years for its generous sizing and patient shop assistants, and went off to park.

As we went in the manageress recognized us and greeted us politely. I thought I saw one of the assistants make hastily towards the staff room but maybe it was time for her coffee break and I was being over sensitive. A chair was pulled up for Rosie and I went to the rail of dresses and picked out a selection in her size. This had her full attention. A dancer in her youth but now crippled with arthritis, she had always loved clothes and had dressed and made up carefully for today's outing.

As she settled on four she wanted to try on, Sally came in to the shop. It was perfect timing.

We helped her into the changing cubicle and I slipped her clothes over her head while Sally took the first dress off the hanger. "No good at all" she declared, "It makes me look much too fat." The second was a good fit. "A little dull but I suppose it would do for everyday" she said. The third was too long and she didn't want to wait for it to be altered, but the fourth, by far the most expensive, was an instant hit, and I think if her body had allowed she would have danced round the shop in order to show it off.

Sally and I had a quick consultation and said we'd go halves on the price of the dress as it could go towards her Christmas present. I maneuvered Rosie back into her clothes while the bill was paid, and we emerged relieved and triumphant ready for a sustaining cup of coffee.

As I was helping her out of the car back into the Care Home she turned to me and said with a smile, "By the way I phoned your daughter-in-law and said she should name the baby Duncan. It was the name of my first boyfriend you know. I can't imagine why they would even think of a name like Zackery."

Strawberries

It's summer time
on Shoreham Beach.
We're eating strawberries
from Sussex or Kent,
the Garden of England.

Memories surface of children
strawberry picking in fields,
eating as they go,
lips stained red with juice.

Strawberries in salads,
smoothies, meringues,
sponges or cheesecake,
covered in cream,
or naked on their own.

The beach, solitary in winter,
is now filled with families.
Children playing on the sand,
Swimmers shivering
as they plunge into the sea.

The taste, the touch, the smell
of barbeques and sun cream.
Shorts and sunhats worn by
tennis players, emulating
Wimbledon stars on
local courts.

When summer time is over,
we'll batten down the hatches
on Shoreham Beach.
Meanwhile we'll
savour the taste,
the touch, the smell,
of strawberries.

The Devil You Know

Julie watched him as he sat in the armchair, newspaper on lap, remote control in one hand. *What is it about men and football?* her last three remarks having met with no response.

The phone rang, and as he didn't move a muscle she went to pick it up. It was Cara. "It's a lovely day, we're having a barbeque. Can you come round?"

"Tom's glued to the football on T.V. but I'd love to. Can I bring anything?" At the thought of some company, Julie felt better already.

"You can bring a bottle if you've got one handy. We've got plenty of food. Come as soon as you like."

When Julie arrived, the party was in full swing. Most of the neighbours she knew already, but there was a new man who came up to her and introduced himself as Justin. *Where did Cara find him he's drop dead gorgeous.* Immediately attentive he got her a drink, asked her all about herself, and before she knew it had led her to a bench seat a little bit away from the others, bringing Julie's bottle of wine with them.

"What's a lovely young woman like you doing all by herself?" he asked, and as the wine loosened her tongue Julie found she was giving full vent to the frustration that had been gradually building up at Tom's lack of attention.

"That's too bad." Justin refilled her glass and casually draped one arm around her shoulders. "Has anyone told you that you have the most beautiful eyes, and the dress you're wearing shows off your figure to perfection? Now tell me more about yourself. Are you one of Cara's neighbours?"

Julie found her glass had emptied again and after refilling it, Justin's hand started to stroke her arm gently, gradually pulling her nearer. As she talked on, it moved down to her waist and then started to move under her dress to squeeze her thigh.

As his face came closer Julie started to pull away, but found herself in a strong grip becoming tighter by the second.

"Oh there you are Julie." Cara came round the corner and Justin's grip loosened abruptly. "I see you've already met Justin. Come and help yourself to some food."

Julie sprang up and gratefully followed Cara to the table in the middle of the garden where the salads were all laid out. "I'm sorry Julie I didn't see you arrive or I would have warned you about him. We call him 'the lech' round here. Can't keep his hands off anything in a skirt."

Feeling humiliated and chastened, Julie ate a plateful of food which acted as blotting paper for the wine, and after chatting to one or two of the neighbours, said her goodbyes and went home.

Tom, still parked in front of the T.V. looked up. "Where have you been? You didn't tell me you were going out. I was worried about you."

"Only round to Cara's for a bit." Julie replied.

The Quiet Road

And so she came to a parting of the ways,
a fork in the road, a choice to make.

Friends called to her,
"Come join us on this path.
We'll travel far and wide.
Hurry, there's no time to waste.
Spectacular sights and sounds
await, dizzying experiences
to amaze and dazzle us
on our adventure."

The still small voice within
showed her the other way.
"Tread gently on this path,
pausing as you go to look around.
Walk quietly among the trees,
take time to watch the flowers grow.
Gaze at the sea, rivers and lakes.
Watch the sun rise and set."

Returning from their journey
her friends told her all they had seen,
and experienced on the way.
But she could not find the words
to tell them why she did not envy them.
For she had chosen the second road
where every day was special,
and the path was
Peace.

Whether you turn to the right or to the left, your ears will hear
a voice behind you saying, "This is the way, walk in it."
Isaiah :30 :21

Made in the USA
Charleston, SC
26 May 2014